Party Talk

ANSWERS TO EVERYDAY LEGAL QUESTIONS FOR TEXAS LAWYERS

AUSTIN 2012

The State Bar of Texas, through its TexasBarBooks Department, publishes practice books prepared and edited by knowledgeable authors to give practicing lawyers as much assistance as possible. The competence of the authors ensures outstanding professional products, but, of course, neither the State Bar of Texas, the editors, nor the authors make either express or implied warranties in regard to their use. Each lawyer must depend on his or her own knowledge of the law and expertise in the use or modification of these materials.

The use of the masculine gender in parts of this book is purely for literary convenience and should, of course, be understood to include the feminine gender as well.

It is not the policy of the State Bar of Texas to assert political positions. It is our hope that this publication fosters healthy discussion about legal issues and the legal profession. Any views expressed in this publication are those of the author and do not necessarily reflect the opinions of the leadership or staff of the Bar.

International Standard Book Number: 978-1-938873-00-3
Library of Congress Control Number: 2012950747

© 2012 State Bar of Texas
Austin, TX 78711

Portions of this book appeared previously in the *Texas Bar Journal*.

Printed in the United States of America

Party Talk Contributors

Joe R. Anderson

Kristy Blanchard

Stephen C. Bolline II

Rebekah Steely Brooker

John Browning

William J. Chriss

Claude Cooke

David Courreges

Aaron M. Dorfner

Lacy Durham

Yolanda Eisenstein

Manuel Escobar

Catherine Evans

Tyler Flood

Leigh N. Ganchan

Stephen Gardner

Katrina Grider

Terry W. Hammond

Wallis Hampton

Kendall Kelly Hayden

Kelli Jones

Gene Major

Michael P. Maslanka

Mandi L. Matlock

Rick McElvaney

Brian McGiverin

Audrey Moorehead

Jana Ortega

Kellie Pai

Bennie M. Ramirez

Elaine Roberts

Matthew M. Sanderson

Grant Scheiner

Shivali Sharma

John W. Shaw

John Sirman

Jonathan E. Smaby

Cindy Smiley

C. Barrett Thomas

Mike Tolleson

TexasBarBooks would like to thank the contributors who made this publication possible. For more information about the authors, see **http://texasbarbooks.net/books/party-talk/**.

STATE BAR OF TEXAS

2012–2013

F.R. "Buck" Files, Jr., *President*

Frank E. Stevenson II, *Chair of the Board*

Deborah J. Bullion, *Chair, Committee on Continuing Legal Education*

Sylvia Cardona, *Chair, Professional Development Subcommittee*

Michelle Hunter, *Executive Director*

TexasBarBooks

Sharon Sandle, *Director*

Jill Hoefling, *Project Manager*

David W. Ashmore, *Publications Attorney*

Lisa T. Chamberlain, *Publications Attorney*

Elma E. Garcia, *Publications Attorney*

Susannah R. Mills, *Publications Attorney*

Sherry Priest, *Publications Attorney*

Vickie Tatum, *Publications Attorney*

Diane Morrison, *Senior Editor*

Michael Ambrose, *Editor*

Courtney Cavaliere, *Editor*

Roger Siebert, *Production Supervisor*

Conor Jensen, *Production and Editorial Assistant*

Isabelle Johnson, *Production and Editorial Assistant*

Jennifer Perez, *Production and Editorial Assistant*

Christopher Sharpe, *Web Content Specialist*

Cynthia Aker, *Meeting Coordinator*

Lara Talkington, *Marketing Coordinator*

Contents

One of the things we lawyers never considered while rereading *To Kill A Mockingbird* during that summer before law school is the fact that, once we passed the bar exam, there was no going back. Being a lawyer is a terminal condition. The only cure is death or disbarment, and most of us would be loath to choose between the two if we ever had to make that decision.

So when you offer a quick bit of your legal expertise at a party (or your kid's soccer game, or the grocery store, or your favorite watering hole), you place yourself squarely under the restrictions of the applicable rules of ethics, no matter how casual your clothes are or how many drinks you've had. Like it or not, we're always lawyers.

Critics of the legal profession who claim that the country is being ruined by "too many lawyers" are apparently unaware of something we know all too well: the world has no shortage of unanswered legal questions. Why is it that when we go to a gathering of any type, we always seem to run into someone who has, inexplicably, never encountered one of our 92,000-and-growing Texas colleagues to answer questions about his son-in-law's DWI arrest or to explain the difference between a living will and the other, um, nonliving kind?

Despite the risks, we usually try to help out with an answer anyway. We do it because, deep down, we lawyers like to use our brains and our experience to help people. There is no better feeling than turning a stranger's look of concern or confusion into one of confidence or understanding simply because we were there to provide the one small piece of context or clarity necessary to make things more clear.

Because you don't know everything that might come up at a party—or in your office, for that matter—your colleagues are here to help you. In the pages that follow, you'll find a wide variety of common legal questions frequently posed by partygoers and clients alike, along with short and succinct answers provided by experts in the field.

Read this book, and you will not only be able to more skillfully navigate the potential pitfalls of dispensing casual advice, but you will also satisfy your urge to help others while providing a positive example of the legal profession in a world that, unfortunately, has too many misconceptions about who we are and what we do.

And isn't that why you became a lawyer in the first place?

— Jonathan E. Smaby
Executive Director
Texas Center for Legal Ethics

Party Talk

Attorney-
Client
Issues

if you give legal advice at a party?

The giving of negligent legal advice at a party can result in liability for the lawyer, although Texas courts are generally quite understanding of the lawyer's plight in these situations. While courts are very reluctant to allow lawyers to be sued for any tort other than malpractice or breach of fiduciary duty, it is conceivable that a lawyer could be sued under the Texas Deceptive Trade Practices–Consumer Protection Act, if the inquirer at the party could show that he detrimentally relied on false advice from the lawyer and was a "consumer," that is, he sought by purchase or lease the lawyer's services, but this would be difficult to show in a cocktail party situation.[1] As for malpractice, generally the existence of an attorney-client relationship is a prerequisite to suit.

Texas courts have said that "A relationship of client and lawyer arises when: (1) a person manifests to a lawyer the person's intent that the lawyer provide legal services for the person; and either: (a) the lawyer manifests to the person consent to do so; or (b) the lawyer fails to manifest lack of consent to do so, and the lawyer knows or reasonably should know that the person reasonably relies on the lawyer to provide the services."[2] Note that the only consent required of the lawyer is that he consent to "provide legal services." Thus one might claim that merely giving the advice manifests a consent to do just that: provide legal services.

This is why malpractice insurers and ethicists recommend sending nonretention letters to those who seek an attorney's services but are rejected. It is also the reason to avoid giving free advice, at cocktail parties or elsewhere. While the lawyer prefacing his remarks with "you understand I am not 'rendering legal services,' am not your lawyer, and you shouldn't rely on this advice" or some such will help, there is always a possibility of a swearing match later as to whether the lawyer was aware the client relied on the lawyer to provide advice but did "nothing to prevent it."

The best way to prevent it is to decline to give the advice, unless the lawyer has such a close relationship with the inquirer that such defensiveness would be both insulting and, under the circumstances, unnecessary. For example, I give my mother free advice all the time because I know she would never sue me and would resent it if I refused.

— ***William J. Chriss, Austin***

1. *Latham v. Castillo*.
2. *MacFarlan v. Nelson*, No. 03-04-00488-CV (Tex. App.—Austin, 2005, citing *Restatement (Third) of the Law Governing Lawyers* § 14 (2000); see also *Bergthold v. Winstead Sechrest & Minick, P.C.*, 2-07-325-CV (Tex. App.—Fort Worth 2009).

I hired a lawyer to represent me, but he won't return my calls.

What can I do?

If your attorney is not returning your calls, the best thing to do is to start documenting your efforts. Begin by sending your attorney a certified letter indicating your concerns. Make sure that you list your questions clearly and give the attorney a deadline to get back with you.

Usually, this will be sufficient to get your attorney's attention. However, if this does not work, you can contact the grievance information hotline at the State Bar of Texas.

You will be greeted by a program associate who will listen to your concerns and give you options that are available through the State Bar's Client-Attorney Assistance Program, a statewide dispute resolution program whose main objective is to assist the public in resolving concerns, disputes, or misunderstanding with Texas lawyers and to facilitate and improve communications between clients and their lawyers.

*— **Bennie M. Ramirez, Austin***

I see commercials from lawyers promising I can win big money lawsuits if I hire them.

Is that true? Is it legal for them to promise that?

There are few attorney advertisements that come out and say that you can win big money. These would not be compliant with the rules, and chances are they have not been filed with the Advertising Review Committee.

Attorneys in Texas need to file their advertisements with the State Bar either before the ad is aired, or concurrently with the airing. If there is a violation, the advertising lawyer needs to either fix the advertisement or stop disseminating the advertisement. With your "win big money" scenario, under the rules attorneys cannot create an unjustified expectation as to your chances of hitting the legal jackpot. In terms of it being "legal" for them to say such a thing, it is a violation of the disciplinary rules and can subject the attorney to the grievance process.

— *Gene Major, Austin*

Can a lawyer represent his family and friends?

One of the more paradoxical aspects of practicing law is that the relatives who most enjoy loudly making fun of your profession at family gatherings are the first ones to call for free advice when they have a legal question or problem. Those are the times when you wish there were a rule that prohibits you from having to even talk to Uncle Charlie.

Alas, there is no express rule prohibiting a lawyer from representing friends or family, but there are many reasons why you should be extra careful in doing so. Even if it feels like a friendly deal, all of the same client-protection rules apply, regardless of whether it is your obnoxious uncle or your beloved mother. Thus, you have to wear your lawyer hat in order to make sure you aren't overlooking anything or letting your guard down.

While many friends and family have a tendency to expect the services for free, experience shows that lawyers too often become neglectful of files that don't produce income, especially when they are busy with paying work. What seemed like a good idea at the time can quickly become a burdensome obligation that leaves you disenchanted. It's also far harder to set the appropriate professional boundaries with people who are in your home or your life and previously have never had to observe such restrictions.

Other potential pitfalls include a lack of objectivity or competence necessary to render quality legal advice. The extent to which you are emotionally involved with the client—and you generally are, one way or the other—can interfere with your legal judgment. Family members also often ask about areas in which you may not practice, such as family law or estate planning, which may seem simple enough on the surface but contain significant hidden dangers.

The best approach is to avoid getting in over your head by handling such inquiries proactively, with a plan in mind. Is this likely to be more involved than it looks? Are you committing to writing a letter or filing something that suggests that you are in for the long haul? Don't let the engagement quietly expand of its own device. Make clear at the outset what you can do and what you can't and reinforce that you reserve the right to refer them to an outside attorney at any time as circumstances develop. It's good to be helpful to your loved ones, but compromising your professional judgment to take a case is not helpful to anyone, especially you.

— *Jonathan E. Smaby, Austin*

I am hearing impaired. I recently needed legal help and contacted three different attorneys. I had difficulty communicating with them, as none of them knew sign language.

How can I get the legal help that I need?

The Americans with Disabilities Act (ADA) requires attorneys to communicate with people with disabilities in a way that they can understand unless doing so would be very difficult or expensive. You need to ask the attorney to obtain the services of a qualified sign language interpreter or use another communication aid to help you understand difficult or lengthy legal information. An attorney cannot charge you for providing an interpreter or other communication aid, but he can ask the judge to pay for qualified interpreters for civil or criminal hearings, trials, or depositions. Hopefully it will not be necessary, but if an attorney still won't provide a qualified sign language interpreter or any other communication aid that you believe you need, even after you have explained the ADA requirement, you can contact the State Bar Client-Attorney Assistance Program to help you access better communication with the attorney.

*— **Elaine Roberts, The Woodlands***

Criminal
Issues

It's 2 A.M. on Saturday, and I've just received a call from the county jail. One of my relatives has been arrested on a criminal matter.

What do I do?

The first thing to do is stay calm so you can think clearly. Your loved one will survive a few hours in the county jail while you plot a course of action. You need to verify what the person has been arrested for. This can be done by calling the jail, the jail's bonding office, or in our bigger counties, visiting the county's Web site. After you have this information, consult an attorney. You can find an attorney by looking through the phone book or by searching the Internet by the name of the county and "jail release." Consult a few of the results and see what your options are.

The county may have a procedure in place in which an attorney can expedite the release of your relative, for a fee of course. If you are unable to reach an attorney, call or visit the jail first thing in the morning and ask the nice officer what the procedures for release are and what you can expect in the next few hours. The jail staff will be happy to help guide you through the process.

During this crisis, remembering to stay calm, listening carefully to the information you are given, and being patient with the system will serve you well while dealing with the booking and bonding process.

— *Jana Ortega, Austin*

I got busted for shoplifting when I was much younger and successfully completed deferred adjudication. However, I have had difficulty getting jobs because it still shows on my record.

How do I remove it?

There are several ways to limit the accessibility of your criminal records by certain private parties. Your record may be expunged pursuant to Texas Code of Criminal Procedure article 45.0216(h) if you were a child when you committed the offense or Texas Code of Criminal Procedure article 55.01(a)(2) if you were an adult and the shoplifting offense was a Class C misdemeanor.

If expunction is not an option, seek an order of nondisclosure from the court that placed you on deferred adjudication pursuant to Texas Government Code section 411.081(d). For more information, download a free copy of the Texas Young Lawyers Association's *Expunctions in Texas* booklet at **tyla.org**.

— *Shivali Sharma, Texarkana*

I treated my client to a nice dinner at his favorite restaurant as a holiday gift. I later found out that on his way home, he was involved in a one-car accident. He was injured, incurred significant costs from medical bills, and was cited for DUI.

Can I be held liable in a civil suit, since I paid for the alcohol?

No. The Texas Dram Shop Act holds that a person or company that is in the business of *selling* alcohol can be held liable for injuries caused by the intoxicated patrons.

Therefore, if your client injures an innocent victim, the victim may have a cause of action against the restaurant, but not likely against you as a social host, unless you recklessly encouraged your client to continue drinking after it was clear that he was drunk.

To maintain your relationship with your client, consider picking him up on the way to dinner, offering to pay for a cab for him on his way home, and limiting the amount of alcohol served during the dinner.

— ***Kendall Kelly Hayden, Dallas***

POINT/COUNTERPOINT:

My city institutes no-refusal weekends around holidays, when those stopped for suspicion of driving while drunk are required to take a blood test.

What should I do if I am stopped for suspicion of driving while intoxicated?

A Defense Lawyer's Take:

First of all, the best advice I can give someone is not to drive if you have had too much to drink. Prosecutors commonly try (improperly, in my opinion) to educate juries that "intoxicated" is a much lower impairment level than "drunk." In Texas, intoxicated for purposes of DWI can be proved any one of three ways: (1) not having the normal use of mental faculties; (2) not having the normal use of physical faculties by reason of the introduction of alcohol, a controlled substance, a dangerous drug, a combination of two or more of those substances, or any other substance into the body; or (3) having an alcohol concentration of 0.08 or more.

Most reasonable people would agree that it is very scary to think that they can have a margarita at dinner and then drive home and be at risk for having a needle stuck in their arm. In my opinion, if an officer merely smells alcohol on a driver's breath, he has pretty much already made up his mind to arrest the driver, regardless of performance on any tests. From a defense viewpoint, the less evidence there is against you, the more difficult it will be for a prosecutor to convict you.

The following tips may help give you a stronger case to defend:

1. If you are being stopped, pull over right away.

2. You can refuse to submit to any of the roadside gymnastics (i.e., standardized field sobriety tests).

3. Don't give a breath specimen. The Intoxilyzer 5000 isn't even warrantied for breath testing by the manufacturer. Additionally, there have been numerous problems with the breath-testing program in Texas. Be aware, though, that a warrant may be obtained for a

sample of your blood. Police agencies are becoming more and more aggressive with no-refusal weekends.

4. Be very polite and ask for a lawyer throughout the investigation (even though the right to counsel may not attach at the scene while under investigation).

Interestingly, one trial court recently threw out a breath test because it found that the officer psychologically coerced the subject to give a breath test by threatening to draw his blood if he refused to blow.

— *Tyler Flood, Houston*

A PROSECUTOR'S PERSPECTIVE:

Many no-refusal jurisdictions will still offer you the opportunity to take a breath test. If you're given the opportunity, take it. A breath test provides immediate results, so if you blow under 0.08 and your arresting officer does not suspect that you are intoxicated on some other substance, you will probably be released with no charge. That means no embarrassing call from jail to your family, no posting a bond, and no court appearances as a criminal defendant.

Also, remember that if you refuse to provide a breath sample after you have been arrested for a DWI offense, your license can be suspended regardless of the final disposition of any criminal charges. While blood tests will also provide definitive results, you and the prosecutors will get the benefit of that information only after the lab analyzes the blood at some later date.

The officer has the discretion to request only a blood sample. It is not your choice. Whether the officer is requesting blood or breath, you will first be asked voluntarily to provide the specimen. If you refuse to provide the requested sample (breath or blood), the officers will work with prosecutors to obtain a blood search warrant signed by a judge or magistrate. That search warrant requires a qualified technician (usually a registered nurse or phlebotomist) to obtain a blood sample. It is no longer a request but a command.

Additionally, your refusal to provide a sample can be considered by a judge or jury as evidence of guilt. My best advice: Make plans to get home safely *before* you start drinking. We all know drinking affects judgment (see also karaoke at office party and late night voice mails to exes). After a few hours of cocktails, rationalizations such as, "It's only a few blocks," "I'm only a little buzzed," or "I can't leave my car in the parking lot" start to sound like good reasons to attempt the drive. They're not! Don't risk your own safety or the safety of the other folks on the road.

Daily we see the consequences of impaired driving, and DWIs are nothing compared with the devastation of intoxication assaults and intoxication manslaughters. The officer that arrests you for DWI may have just saved your life or someone else's life. Please take a cab or designate a driver.

— *Catherine Evans, Houston*

Road
Rules

Is it legal to text while driving?

OMG, I can't believe u would ask me that!! While Texas does not currently have a law banning all drivers from texting, drivers under the age of eighteen are prohibited from using wireless communication devices (which would include texting devices), except in cases of emergency. Tex. Transp. Code § 545.424(a)(2).

With limited exceptions, drivers may not use a wireless communication device within school crossing zones. Tex. Transp. Code § 545.424(b).

There are also various city ordinances throughout Texas relating to "distracted driving"—so be careful! LOL. :)

— *Grant Scheiner, Houston*

Can people sit in the bed of a truck if we aren't on a paved road?

Possibly. The fine-only law relating to "Riding in Open Beds" applies to drivers who have a child younger than eighteen years of age in the bed of a truck or trailer. Tex. Transp. Code § 545.414(a). There are several defenses to prosecution, including that the driver was operating the vehicle to transport farm workers from one field to another on a farm-to-market road, ranch-to-market road, or county road outside of a municipality. Tex. Transp. Code § 545.414(c). It is also a defense that the driver was operating or towing the vehicle in a parade or in an emergency, operating the vehicle on a beach, operating a vehicle that is the only vehicle owned or operated by members of the household, or operating the vehicle in a hayride permitted by the governing body of or law enforcement agency of each county or municipality in which the hayride occurs. *Id.* Six words to remember: "Officer, we're on an official hayride!"

— **Grant Scheiner, Houston**

Do my passengers have to wear seat belts while riding in the back seat?

Yes. A person violates Texas's seat belt law if the person is at least fifteen years of age, is riding in a passenger vehicle while the vehicle is operated, is occupying a seat that is equipped with a safety belt, and is not secured by a safety belt. Tex. Transp. Code § 545.413(a). So click it or ticket!

— *Grant Scheiner, Houston*

Business
Issues

I really enjoy making cupcakes for my friends and coworkers. I've been doing brisk business and filling more orders.

At what point should I become incorporated or a company?

As with so many legal questions, it depends. It is a cost-benefit analysis. The benefit potentially could be substantial.

By incorporating, you can protect your personal assets from claims made against the business—for example, if someone claims a cupcake made him or her sick or that you failed to fill an important order.

Generally, the more assets you have to protect and the more likely it is that your customers will make a claim against the business, the more important it will be to incorporate. The costs can vary greatly. The initial monetary cost, particularly for a one-person corporation or limited liability company, is relatively low; having an attorney help you form one should cost somewhere around one thousand dollars (including filing fees). There may be additional tax costs, but these can be lessened by using an LLC or an S corporation.

Finally, there are ongoing administrative burdens associated with a corporation or LLC, such as filing separate tax returns, keeping separate accounting records, making sure to sign checks and contracts in the name of the business, and having corporate meetings.

If the benefits outweigh the costs or if they are close, you should consider incorporating.

— *Manuel Escobar, Austin*

I invested in my friend's small business. Now my friend won't talk to me about the business or my investment.

What should I do?

First, do you have anything in writing? Typically the documentation will control the nature of the investment and the investor's legal rights.

Second, what were the terms of the investment? Was it a loan, an equity investment, or something else? If it was a loan, what were the key terms (for example, interest rate, loan maturity)? If it was an equity investment, what was the form of investment?

Shareholders, for instance, have certain statutory and common-law rights independent of their contract rights, including the right to receive basic information about the business. And your friend must run the business for the benefit of all shareholders. Some Texas courts have also allowed minority shareholders to bring shareholder oppression claims if the majority shareholder engages in certain types of misconduct. While partners enjoy similar protections, remember that partners in general partnerships can be personally liable for partnership debts.

If your friend continues to stonewall you and you think you may have a significant amount of money at stake, then you should seriously consider hiring a lawyer.

— *Wallis Hampton, Houston*

I am thinking about opening a small business.

Do I have to buy worker's compensation insurance?

Should I buy worker's compensation insurance?

Texas is the only state where having worker's compensation insurance is not mandatory. A business can "opt out" of the worker's compensation system.

Whether a business should purchase worker's compensation insurance is a decision that is best made with the assistance of an attorney and insurance professional. If a business has worker's compensation, it is protected from most lawsuits by workers for on-the-job injuries since receiving worker's compensation benefits is the "exclusive remedy" of the worker. This is often called "the shield." However, there are insurance products out there that are not worker's compensation policies that provide disability and medical benefits to injured workers that some business owners find more cost effective for their businesses.

Be mindful, though—a company without "the shield" provided by worker's compensation insurance is not protected from a negligence lawsuit by the worker, who only needs to prove some negligence on the employer's part. This is called "going bare."

Ultimately, the business decision of whether to have "the shield" or "go bare" should be made carefully with input from your attorney and insurance agent.

— *Joe R. Anderson, Austin*

I own a hotel. A well-known Web site that publishes reviews of hotels and restaurants recently published a review of my business that is false, contains curse words, and is affecting the number of customers who want to stay at my hotel.

Is there anything I can do to get the reviewer and the Web site to remove the post?

Under the Communications Decency Act, owners of an "interactive computer service" (ICS) (for example, Yelp!) who publish information provided by others are not liable for defamatory statements made about another unless the owner actively engages in the gathering of information from the reviewer that leads to the defamatory statement.

Therefore, you are unlikely to get legal redress from the ICS owner. Focus instead on the reviewer. In contrast to an ICS owner, any person who makes a defamatory statement about another on an ICS site can be held personally liable for his or her statements. Remember, you can respond to the review on most ICS sites.

If that doesn't work, send a demand letter to the reviewer asking them to remove the defamatory post and seek appropriate legal action.

— *Kendall Kelly Hayden, Dallas*

Property
Issues

I'm a homeowner.
I recently discovered a
construction defect.

What is the window of
time in which I can sue
the builder?

There are two things you need to consider.

The first, which immediately comes to an attorney's mind, is the statute of limitations. The statute of limitations establishes a time limit for a person to file a lawsuit and is subject to the discovery rule, which causes the clock to start ticking once a person discovers the facts giving rise to his claim.

The second thing to consider, and this may not immediately come to mind, is the statute of repose. *See* Tex. Civ. Prac. & Rem. Code § 16.009. Under the statute of repose, you have ten years from substantial completion of the house to sue a builder. There is no discovery rule with statute of repose, so your claim is barred ten years after the house is substantially complete. This can result in an owner's claim against the builder being barred by the statute of repose even though the statute of limitations clock has not started to tick. Seems harsh, but it is true.

*— **Stephen C. Bolline II, Dallas***

I have almost a year left on my apartment lease, but want to take three months off to go backpack around Europe. My buddy from high school got evicted from his place, and I want to sublet to him for the three months until he finds a new place, then move back in when I get back.

Can I do that?

Absent a provision in your lease to the contrary, Texas law states that during the term of your lease, you may not rent the leasehold to any other person without the prior consent of the landlord.

If your lease does not give you the right to sublet, you should contact your landlord to obtain permission to sublet to your friend.

Even if your landlord allows you to sublet to your friend, you would still be liable under the lease for any rent your friend fails to pay during the sublet term.

*— **Rick McElvaney, Houston***

The house we are renting was foreclosed on, and the bank has given us until the end of the month to move out, despite the fact that we have ten months left on the lease.

What can we do?

You are protected by the Protecting Tenants at Foreclosure Act of 2009, which states that, in the case of any foreclosure on a federally related mortgage loan or on any dwelling or residential real property, the bank assumed its interest subject to the rights of any bona fide tenant on the date of foreclosure.

Tenants in this situation must be given at least ninety days' notice to vacate and may have the right to occupy the premises until the end of their lease term. If you were renting without a lease or with a lease terminable at will under state law, you would be entitled to ninety days' notice to vacate.

— Rick McElvaney, Houston

With all the talk about water supplies and water shortages, would it be okay for me to find my own sources of water?

Do I own the water in the creek that runs across my land?

Can I drill a water well and use that water?

These are great questions, and they highlight the important difference between surface water and groundwater ownership in Texas. That creek water, as surface water in a watercourse, is owned by the state of Texas. Unless it fits within an exemption, the right to use surface water requires the state's permission. The Texas Commission on Environmental Quality's Web site (**tceq.texas.gov**) is an excellent source of information on this topic.

And what about the water well? That's a deep subject! Joking aside, the issue of groundwater ownership is a serious matter in Texas, and the Texas Supreme Court issued a much-anticipated opinion on this issue on February 24, 2012: *Edwards Aquifer Authority v. Day*. Generally, the court held that groundwater is owned in place, with consideration of the law of capture and police regulations.

The constitutional claim of a "taking" by the groundwater authority was remanded for further evidentiary development. Meanwhile, if you want to drill a water well, you would be wise to check local laws and ordinances to determine whether your property is within the boundaries of a groundwater conservation district (which may require a well registration or permit) and to use a licensed driller for the work.

— *Cindy Smiley, Austin*

I own a ranch, but I don't own the minerals.

An oil company told me it is going to drill a well and cut a road right through my pasture.

Can they do that?

Yes, they can. The mineral estate (which includes the oil and gas underneath the surface) is the dominant estate. That means the mineral estate owner, or, in this case, his or her lessee, has the right to use as much of the surface as may be reasonably necessary to develop the minerals by drilling its well. This includes selecting its drilling location in your pasture, cutting a road through the pasture, and even using your caliche to build its road and drill site. Subject to some narrow exceptions, the oil company even has the right to interfere with your use of the ranch. But, if you interfere with the oil company's operations, you could be liable for damages.

— *Aaron M. Dorfner, Midland*

I try to keep up with the news and current events, including the topic of hydraulic fracturing and hydrocarbon recovery, but what on earth are people talking about when they refer to fracing or fracking?

First, let's discuss how to write the name of the process. Industry refers to "fracing." The press came up with "fracking" in recent years. The grammatically correct name would be the contraction "frac'ing," wouldn't it? Perhaps an English major can confirm this for us.

However, to get to the technology, you may be interested to learn that hydraulic fracturing is not a new technology; patents for the process were filed in 1947. The first two commercial fracturing treatments of wells were in 1949—in Oklahoma and Texas on the same day. Basically, hydraulic fracturing is a process in which fluid is pumped into a well at a high rate, such that the hydraulic pressure of the fluid causes the rock around the well to fracture. The amount of hydraulic pressure required to fracture (or "frac") the rock varies in different parts of the world, but in Texas it is often about 7/10ths of a pound of pressure per foot of depth of the well (7,000 pounds per square inch (psi) for a 10,000 foot well).

After the fracture is formed by pumping fluid, more fluid is pumped with sand or similar material in the fluid. When pumping stops, the sand is left in the fracture and oil or gas can flow into the well much faster than before. In fact, most wells could not be drilled in modern times if hydraulic fracturing were not available—the wells would not produce at a high enough rate to justify drilling them.

In very recent years, the hydraulic fracturing that was used for *vertical wells* has been combined with a new technology, horizontal drilling, to make possible a revolution in oil and gas production. A *horizontal well* may go down vertically for a few thousand feet and then turn and extend a mile or more horizontally. It is drilled through a rock called a "shale" that contains large amounts of hydrocarbons that previously could not be produced at an economical rate.

The drill bit going horizontally through the shale rock is steered using precise and sophisticated technology. Hydraulic fractures are then formed by pumping fluid down the well to enter the shale formation through perforations located within the horizontal pipe, often at intervals of 200 to 500 feet. The fractures extend outward from the horizontal well and create a very large area that can collect hydrocarbons and allow them to flow to the well.

This combination of hydraulic fracturing and horizontal drilling technologies has been a game-changer in the energy business. The technology proven in Texas is being applied to shale rocks in many parts of the world, and no doubt the technology will continue to expand for many years.

— *Claude Cooke, Conroe*

Family
Issues

My ex has stopped paying child support.

Can I prevent my ex from visiting our child?

No. The nonpayment of child support is not a defense to violating a court order with regard to possession and access of a child. If there is a court order granting a conservator of a child the right to exercise possession and access with the child, a failure to deliver the child as ordered would constitute a violation of that court order that could result in the noncomplying conservator being held in contempt.

Under the Texas Family Code section 157.007, the only statutory defenses for failure to comply with an order for possession or access to a child are—

1. the involuntary inability to comply with the order and
2. the voluntary relinquishment of actual possession and control of the child by the conservator who has the right to possession under the order.

If a conservator of a child wants to modify the possession schedule of a child with another conservator, they have the right to file a motion to modify with the court and seek a modification. However, until the prior order is modified by the court, it is still a valid and enforceable order.

— *Kristy Blanchard, Plano*

I recently lost my job and cannot afford to pay my child support.

Can I lower the amount of child support I am paying?

Probably.

A court may modify a child support order if the circumstances of a child or a person affected by the order have materially and substantially changed since the date the last order was entered. A material and substantial change could be a change in income or a loss of employment.

If the loss of employment was not voluntary and no income is being earned, the court could modify the child support down to an amount that would be paid by an obligor who was earning minimum wage. If the loss of income was voluntary, the court may not modify the child support at all.

If the court finds that the actual income of the obligor is significantly less than what the obligor could earn because of intentional unemployment or underemployment, the court may calculate child support based on the earning potential of the obligor by looking at what kind of income the obligor has made in the past.

*— **Kristy Blanchard, Plano***

My elderly mother, who suffers from dementia, has been declining in health for some time.

Do I need to become her legal guardian?

Come on over, and let's have a burger and a drink. This doesn't happen in real life the same way it does in the movies. To avoid the guardianship, you need to find out if your mom has previously signed powers of attorney. If she did, you can probably avoid a guardianship because she named her agents while she was still OK. If she doesn't have powers of attorney and the doctor says she can't sign documents now, then you need to do the guardianship.

Here's how it works . . . [Two hours later] So, go find those documents and see what the doctor says. Boy, you sure know how to have fun at a party!

— *Terry W. Hammond, El Paso*

I am twenty-nine years old and recently married a seventy-nine year-old oil tycoon. He has five children by his ex-wives. His children told me he doesn't need a will because I get everything since Texas is a "community property" state.

Are they telling me the truth?

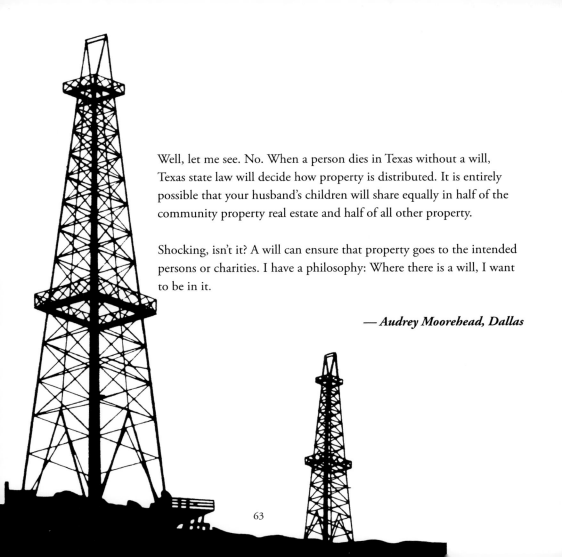

Well, let me see. No. When a person dies in Texas without a will, Texas state law will decide how property is distributed. It is entirely possible that your husband's children will share equally in half of the community property real estate and half of all other property.

Shocking, isn't it? A will can ensure that property goes to the intended persons or charities. I have a philosophy: Where there is a will, I want to be in it.

— *Audrey Moorehead, Dallas*

How does a U.S. citizen or permanent resident bring a family member to the United States?

You will first need to file a "petition for alien relative," which proves the type of relationship (for example, parent, spouse, child, or sibling) between you and your family member.

After the approval of this petition, your family member will be notified by the National Visa Center when a visa number is available (which ranges from zero to eight years or more, depending on type of relationship and country of birth) and what documents to prepare.

Then, your family member needs to attend an interview at an U.S. Consulate, and, after the immigrant visa is approved, he or she will have six months to enter the United States.

— *Kellie Pai, Houston*

Since Texas is a no-fault state, does that mean that it does not matter if my spouse has had an affair or is at fault in the breakup of our marriage?

No. The fact that Texas is a no fault state means that in Texas, parties can get divorced without having to plead any fault in the breakup of the marriage.

The parties can merely plead that the marriage has become insupportable due to discord or conflict of personalities that destroys the legitimate ends of the marriage relationship as grounds for their divorce.

Further, the court can take into consideration fault in the breakup of the marriage when dividing the marital assets between the parties in a just and right division.

Therefore, if there has been an affair by one spouse that led to the breakup of the marriage, the court could order that the innocent spouse receive more of the community assets in the divorce.

— *Kristy Blanchard, Plano*

I have been taking care of my mom's finances since she executed her power of attorney two years ago, but she recently passed away.

As I hold her power of attorney, what must I do to settle her estate?

Nothing. When your mom passed away, her power of attorney became invalid, and your appointment as her agent expired. You should help locate your mother's last will and testament or living trust to determine who she named the executor or trustee.

The executor of your mother's will or the trustee of her living trust is the person legally responsible for settling your mother's estate.

— *Rebekah Steely Brooker, Dallas*

I have a living will in place.

Is that different than a regular will?

Yes, a living will and a regular will are different, and I would encourage you to have both.

A living will is also known as a "directive to physician," and it becomes effective only if medically necessary while the individual who executed it is still alive. A living will instructs your physician and other medical personnel to either withhold or continue life-sustaining procedures in the event you are in a terminal or irreversible medical condition and unable to make your own medical decisions.

A regular will—more specifically called a last will and testament—does not become effective until after the individual who executed it passes away. The will is the legal declaration of how an individual wants his estate disposed of following his death.

— *Rebekah Steely Brooker, Dallas*

Employment
Issues

I recently got laid off from my job after working there for the last two years. I went to rollover my 401(k) balance to an individual IRA account, but I realized my employer did not give me my company match.

How can my employer keep the company match that was promised to me?

You should request a copy of your 401(k) plan document from your former employer and check the vesting rules. Some plans allow you to fully (100 percent) vest as soon as you join the plan. Other rules require you to complete a number of years of service before you are fully vested.

By law, all participants must be fully vested after six years of service. Other special rules allow you to become fully vested if you reach the state retirement age (usually sixty-five), become disabled, die, or if the plan is terminated.

If you are laid off before you are fully vested, it is possible to lose the company match.

— Lacy Durham, Dallas

I have heard a lot lately about states and the federal government wanting employers to verify their employees' work authorization status.

Can't I just recruit only U.S. citizens to simplify the process?

Except in very specific circumstances, you should not ask whether a job applicant is a U.S. citizen or "green card" holder before making an offer of employment—this includes advertising for "U.S. citizens only." It is illegal for employers to discriminate with respect to hiring, firing, or recruitment or referral for a fee, based on an individual's citizenship or immigration status. Unless you are required to do so by law, regulation, executive order, or government contract, you cannot implement a U.S. citizen– or lawful permanent residents–only hiring policy.

However, you can put applicants on notice about the employment eligibility verification requirement by including a statement on the job application form that explains your posthire obligation to verify identity and eligibility to work in the United States by means of the I-9 form. You can also generally inquire whether job applicants are "legally authorized to work." This must be asked of *every* job applicant, however, to avoid problems under antidiscrimination laws.

— *Leigh N. Ganchan, Houston*

My office doesn't give me religious holidays off.

Can I take them anyway?

Title VII of the Civil Rights Act of 1964 requires employers to make "reasonable accommodations" for employees' religious practices, but they don't have to make accommodations that are expensive or highly disruptive. A reasonable accommodation for holidays might be flexible scheduling or the option to take unpaid leave.

Talk to your boss. Before an employer has to do anything, you have to alert him or her to the need for accommodation. If you can't come to an agreement, it would be smarter to file a claim with the Equal Employment Opportunity Commission than to take off without permission.

— *Brian McGiverin, Austin*

Neighbor
Issues

My neighbor's dog viciously attacked my cat in my backyard.

Can I have the dog put down?

Whether or not the dog can be put down, or euthanized, is likely to be determined by ordinance. Some ordinances include the possibility of euthanasia for animal-on-animal atte... Some do not.

Make sure you know your local ordinances regarding animals. As for what you can do personally, state law says that, under certain circumstances, you can kill a dog that "is attacking" or "has recently attacked" a domestic animal on your property.

However, it might not be a good idea to kill your neighbor's dog. There may have been extenuating circumstances.

— *Yolanda Eisenstein, Dallas*

...ows have been entering my ...though the woods behind our house at night, then are gone in the morning. I've contacted farmers in the area, but nobody has claimed the cows. I would like to pen them so that we can call the sheriff's department out to investigate.

Is it illegal to pen livestock that are not yours?

To many urban Texans, the concept of an "estray," most commonly a loose horse or cow, is unimaginable. It has been a long time since a Hereford bull walked unattended up Congress Avenue in downtown Austin. However, with the long-term trend of urban encroachment on traditional agricultural communities, it's time for urban and suburban Texans to educate themselves on what to do when they find a cow eating their petunias.

If you do not know who the owner is, chapter 142 of the Agriculture Code requires the owner of private property to report an estray to the sheriff "as soon as reasonably possible." Though the Code is silent on the issue of capture, unless the animal is dangerous, law enforcement agencies encourage property owners to corral an estray to prevent the potential of serious public safety issues, such as if the animal were to wander onto a busy road.

Worried about the cost of caring for your newly captured estray? Not to worry! The Code provides that the owner may redeem the animal from the property owner after payment of fees and damages.

*— **David Courreges, Austin***

My neighbor plays loud music and has parties every weekend that last late into the night. I've tried to talk to him about it but he just thinks I'm an old fogey.

What recourse do I have?

The good news is you likely do have some remedial courses of action you can pursue. The bad news is that none of them are going to make you better friends with your rock-star neighbors, nor get you an invite to their next "killer" party.

My first bit of advice would be to politely but sternly ask your neighbor one more time. You may have to live next to this whippersnapper for a long time. You want to make sure you did everything you could to keep the relationship cordial before resorting to legal measures.

On the other hand, if the pleasantries have failed, you should first turn to local law enforcement. Most municipalities have ordinances relating to noise, and officers can issue citations for ordinance violations. Ordinances vary from town to town, so you'll have to check with your police department or city hall to know the details of your local rules. Take heart though! Playing artists like Justin Bieber in public is almost universally banned regardless of volume or time of day.

Finally, you can pursue civil action if you find it necessary and law enforcement can't or won't help. Noise, if sufficiently extreme, may constitute a nuisance as courts have determined it can interfere with the "quiet enjoyment" of your land. This is potentially an expensive and time consuming alternative though. Sometimes you just have to hear Katy Perry and Slayer at 5,000 decibels at midnight to learn to appreciate them.

— C. Barrett Thomas, Abilene

Copyright
Issues

I work at a publication and receive review copies of movies, CDs, and books.

Once I am finished with them, can I give them away or sell them?

You can give them away or sell them if ownership of the copy has passed to you personally and not the publication that employs you. Also, the company sending the review copy may want to control the date of release to the public in which case premature distribution by the reviewer could impair relations with the source of the copy.

The "First Sale Doctrine" under the U.S. copyright law gives the copyright owner the exclusive right to distribute the copyrighted work to the public by sale or other transfer of ownership. However, once an authorized copy has been sold or given away so that ownership is transferred to another, the new owner can dispose of that copy by sale or gift (but not rental if the work is a sound recording).

— *Mike Tolleson, Austin*

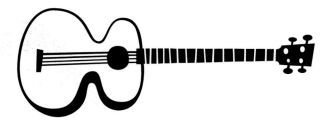

I want to print out a picture I found on the Internet, to put on invitations.

Do I need to pay to use the image?

The person who created the picture owns a copyright in it, and you need his or her permission before using it—even for an invitation. The best approach is to look for pictures in places that allow you to easily obtain a license to use them.

You can find royalty-free images and buy licenses on sites such as **istockphoto.com** or **gettyimages.com**. You can also search for images at **flickr.com/creativecommons**, which has millions of photos with a "creative commons" license, allowing you to use the images for noncommercial use. For information on the basics of copyrights, visit **www.copyright.gov**.

*— **John Sirman, Austin***

Social Media
& Internet
Issues

Can I Google job applicants?

The short and practical answer is no. Why? The liability risks far outweigh the minimal benefits of obtaining any particularly relevant, accurate, or job-related information. A good best practice to follow is this: if you cannot ask about it an interview, then you cannot find out about it via social media or online search engines. In the context of pre-employment inquiries, an "Internet applicant search" is defined as the use of such social media and online search engines as Google, Bing, Safari, Facebook, LinkedIn, MySpace, Friendster, Twitter, YouTube, blogs, Web logs, texts, instant messaging, e-mail, Skype, online commentary, and chat rooms to conduct background checks and references. There are several compelling reasons why employers should be wary of Internet applicant searches.

First, Internet searches often reveal information about an applicant's protected status, for example, race, sex, national origin, age, disability or handicap, sexual orientation or preference, veteran status, religion, or pregnancy, simply because many people leave their social media profiles public and do not restrict access to photos and other self-identifying information. Title VII, ADA, ADAAA, ADEA,[1] and many states (including Texas) prohibit employers from making pre-employment inquiries that are designed to reveal or disclose such protected status or information. Furthermore, FMLA, GINA, and HIPAA[2] prohibit employers from unlawfully obtaining information about an applicant's medical history or condition, sick leave use, or other confidential health information via an Internet search. Finally, the National Labor Relations Act prohibits employers from finding out about an applicant's union membership, organizing activities, or other concerted and protected activities. The bottom line is that employers may obtain information during an Internet search that applicants might later assume is the basis for harassment, discrimination, retaliation, or another adverse employment action. The critical problem is this: once the employer knows the personal information, it cannot "unring the bell." This potential liability is why human resources professionals are very concerned about these issues.

Second, while it appears that employers have unlimited access to Internet information, employers must understand that these alleged Internet "treasure troves" often contain information that is inaccurate, misleading, out of context, or flat-out wrong. For example, Facebook recently reported that approximately 83 million (8.7 percent) out of its 955 million user accounts are

1. Title VII of the Civil Rights Act of 1964, the Americans with Disabilities Act, the Americans with Disabilities Act Amendments Act, the Age Discrimination in Employment Act.

2. Family and Medical Leave Act, Genetic Information Discrimination Act of 2008, Health Insurance Portability and Accountability Act of 1996.

duplicate, misclassified, and "undesirable" account profiles.[3] In addition, most people today have "computer twins," that is, people online with the same name and date of birth. Employers cannot always be sure that what they see online actually refers to the applicant in question or is even close to being true.

Third, social media and online searches clearly meet the definition of "third party investigative consumer reports" under the Fair Credit Reporting Act (FCRA) which is enforced by the Federal Trade Commission (FTC). In a recent blog, the FTC stated that background checks using information obtained through either online search engines or social media sites must follow the same FCRA rules that apply to the more traditional information that employers have used in the past.[4] This means that employers must have the applicant's written consent and must provide express FCRA disclosures before such online inquiries are initiated.

— *Katrina Grider, Cypress*

3. Heather Kelly, *83 Million Facebook Accounts Are Fakes and Dupes*, CNNTech (2012), at **http://www.cnn .com/2012/08/02/tech/social-media/facebook-fake-accounts/index.html**.

4. FTC *Business Center Blog*, "The Fair Credit Reporting Act & Social Media: What Businesses Should Know" (June 23, 2011), at **http://business.ftc.gov/blog/2011/06/fair-credit-reporting-act-social-media-what-businesses-should-know**.

No Googling of applicants? Really? I thought everyone was doing it.

In 2011, the Society for Human Resource Management (SHRM) conducted a study finding that, contrary to popular belief, only 26 percent of companies used online search engines to screen applicants and only 18 percent of companies used social networking sites for that purpose.[1] The study also indicated that employers listed the following reasons (among others) for not screening applicants on the Internet:

- Legal risks due to concerns about discovering protected status information (66 percent)
- Information found is unreliable (48 percent)
- Information is not job-related (45 percent)

The study further stated that of the small percentage of companies that use information from online search engines (26 percent) or social networking Web sites (18 percent) to screen candidates, few have actually used this information to disqualify job candidates. Only 15 percent of this group indicated that they used online search engine information to disqualify job candidates, while 30 percent used social networking Web site information to disqualify job candidates.

— *Katrina Grider, Cypress*

1. SHRM, *SHRM Survey Findings: The Use of Social Networking Websites and Online Search Engines in Screening Job Candidates* (Aug. 25, 2011), at **http://www.shrm.org/Research/SurveyFindings/Articles/Pages/TheUseofSocialNetworkingWebsitesandOnlineSearchEnginesinScreeningJobCandidates.aspx**.

I've applied for a job and the company asked for my Facebook password.

Can they do that?

No, employers should not, under any circumstances, ask applicants for their Facebook passwords. Such requests violate privacy laws as well as the Stored Communications Act (SCA) and Computer Fraud Abuse Act (CFAA). The SCA prohibits unauthorized intentional access to electronic information, and the CFAA prohibits unauthorized intentional access to a computer to obtain information. Congress currently is considering legislation that would prohibit employers from soliciting social media account passwords. Maryland recently banned the practice.

*— **Katrina Grider, Cypress***

Can I get fired for complaining about my boss on Facebook?

Like a lot in the law, "it depends." The National Labor Relations Act (NLRA) protects an employee who complains about working conditions (even if there is no union) if—and this is a BIG if—she does it in concert with other employees. So, if she says on her Facebook page that she talked with others employees and they all believe that the boss treats them badly regarding working conditions, she is protected from termination. But if she just pops off on her own, the employer can terminate her without running afoul of the NLRA. Still, many unresolved questions remain.

If employee A complains on Facebook about the boss and the working conditions he imposes, and Employee B hits the FB "Like" feature, is that engaging in protected activity?

Wait, there's more. Public employees have a First Amendment right to protest about matters of public concern and be protected from retaliation. That right is not lost merely because the employees does so on his FB page. Remember: FB is the new town square. But there are traditional legal limits; the comments made by employees in either the NLRA or First Amendment contexts must be stated in a civil manner. Protection can be lost if they are not.

Finally, there are limits. Check out the case of an employee who posted on her FB page that her company was not paying her overtime under the Fair Labor Standards Act. She claimed she was terminated as a result of the FB post. The court tossed the lawsuit, saying that FLSA antiretaliation protections only extend to employees who file a complaint under the FLSA and a FB post is not a "filing" under the law. Yes, FB is new and different but the traditional legal principles apply. The more things change, the more they remain the same.

— *Michael P. Maslanka, Dallas*

My child posted inappropriate photos to his Facebook page. School administrators are threatening to suspend him.

Can they do that?

It depends. In more than one federal case, courts have tried to balance a student's First Amendment rights with school administrators' mission of maintaining order and discipline in the school. While at least one appellate court sided with the educators in the matter of a social networking page that was promoting unlawful behavior, most have upheld a student's freedom of speech, even though it might be considered inappropriate and/or critical of, or even derogatory toward, teachers.

While school administrators' efforts at suppressing student expression have been upheld where the students' activities were materially and substantially disrupting the work and discipline of the school, the potential for disruption is usually harder to show when the expression in question happens off-campus. And if the student's social networking profile is privacy-restricted (as opposed to publicly viewable), the school's legal justification is even weaker. But there are circumstances where photos or statements appearing in cyberspace could pose a legitimate concern for school officials; for example, threats of violence made on a Facebook page would certainly be viewed as relevant to school safety.

— John Browning, Dallas

Consumer
Issues

I've just had a money judgment entered against me. How long before the other side can collect on it, and what are my options if I don't pay the whole amount?

Assuming that no postjudgment motions or appeals have been filed, the judgment of the court becomes final thirty days after the order was signed. In most circumstances the thirty days must pass before a judgment creditor can attempt to collect from you. Therefore, you should be clear until day thirty-one.

That being said, as with almost all legal matters, there are some exceptions. A judgment creditor may seek an abstract of judgment immediately after the order is signed in an effort to collect on the judgment. Once an abstract of judgment is filed and recorded, it creates a lien on all of your real property not protected by the homestead exemption. Additionally, a judgment creditor can immediately begin postjudgment discovery processes and attempt to obtain information about your assets that may be subject to recovery to satisfy the judgment. Don't ignore these requests. Admissions can be deemed against you for collection of the judgment just as they could have been deemed against you in the initial lawsuit.

All judgments of a court must be enforced by execution or other appropriate means. Therefore, the judgment creditor is limited to the collection methods outlined by Texas law. This could include executions (enforcement of the judgment by seizing and selling your nonexempt property), garnishments (property in possession of another person that is owed to you is intercepted to satisfy the judgment) and turnovers and receiverships (same thing as execution but reserved for more difficult property).

The best way to avoid all of the above is to attempt to work out a reasonable settlement with the judgment creditor. Judgment creditors only want to have the judgment and costs satisfied. Therefore, as long as you are making an attempt to work with them, they may be amenable to working out payment arrangements. Remember to get those payment arrangements in writing including full amount, payment terms, and where the payment is to be made. Only make those payments in a form that you can track, for example, a money order or cashier's check. Be sure that you keep track of every payment by sending it certified mail, return receipt requested, or by another form that indicates receipt by the judgment creditor.

Most importantly, don't forget to get an acknowledgment or release of judgment as soon as you have finished paying what you agreed to pay to satisfy the judgment.

— *John W. Shaw, Fort Worth*

at work?

Under Texas law, as long as the debt collector isn't oppressing, harassing, or abusing the caller, there is nothing that prohibits a debt collector from calling you at work. However, where Texas law does not protect, the federal law does.

The federal Fair Debt Collections Practices Act (FDCPA) was created to eliminate abusive debt collection practices by debt collectors. There are several provisions within the FDCPA you can use to your advantage to prevent a debt collector from calling you at work. Unfortunately, the old adage "verbal agreements are not worth the paper they are written on" is applicable and to prevent them from calling you at work, you must notify them in writing.

In your written notice, tell the debt collector that being called at work is inconvenient. Sounds simple, but the FDCPA prohibits a debt collector from contacting you at any place that they know is inconvenient to you. The alternative is to let the debt collector know that your employer prohibits you from receiving these types of phone calls at work. This reason can be used by itself or in addition to the prior notice.

Finally, if you want to cease all calls from the collector, include in your letter that you wish the debt collector to cease further communication with you. At that point, the debt collector can only communicate with you to advise you that they are ceasing any further efforts to collect from you and also to advise you that they may seek other remedies to collect the unpaid debt. Therefore, you should be careful with this option because it may speed up the timeline in which the debt collector files a lawsuit against you to recover the unpaid debt.

To make sure that you have proof that you have notified the debt collector in writing you should—

1. make a copy of your correspondence;

2. mail the original by certified mail, return receipt requested; and

3. keep the copy forever.

If a debt collector violates the FDCPA, they may be liable to you for civil penalties. Remember, the only way that you can prove they violated the FDCPA though, is to have evidence of such violations.

— *John W. Shaw, Fort Worth*

I received a notice about a class-action suit that I will be included in unless I opt out.

What should I do?

If I had a nickel for every time I've gotten a notice about a class action . . . well, I'd have a bunch of nickels. The notice is probably sent after a settlement. What you will want to do mostly depends on whether you have any real claims of your own against the defendant.

If you have your own claims of any kind against the same defendant or if you are in a continuing relationship with the defendant (such as having a loan from a bank or a utilities account), then you should probably opt out as instructed by the notice.

If you don't opt out, you will remain a part of the lawsuit, which will release claims you might have against that defendant. Of course, if you stand to get hundreds of dollars if you don't opt out, that's a different matter. But, most likely, you'll have to file a claim form just to receive a relatively small amount of money, and only you can decide whether it's worth it.

If the settlement is junk, you can also choose to remain part of the lawsuit, but file an objection to the settlement—the notice should tell you how to do that.

— *Stephen Gardner, Dallas*

I graduated from college two years ago but still haven't found a good job. My student loan payments are killing me.

If I file for bankruptcy, will my student loan debt be discharged?

You know that old saying about taxes and death? They should really change it to "student loans and death." Even federal income taxes are easier to discharge in bankruptcy than student loans these days!

While bankruptcy is a good option to reduce or eliminate most other consumer debts, student loans are generally nondischargeable. They can be discharged if you prove "undue hardship," but you'd pretty much better be totally and permanently disabled if you want to succeed. To prove undue hardship in Texas, you need to prove that you absolutely cannot pay now *or in the future*, that the circumstances causing you to be unable to pay weren't present when you obtained the loans, and that none of it is in any way your fault or within your control. Sound tough? It really is. While discharges of student loans do appear to be on the rise, they are still relatively rare and hard-fought.

The better plan is to apply for a Direct Consolidation Loan through the U.S. Department of Education and take advantage of their "Income-Based Repayment" option. Under IBR, payments are capped at 15 percent of what you earn over 150 percent of federal poverty guidelines. And starting in 2013, payments for more recent borrowers will be capped at 10 percent. The best part? After twenty-five years of on-time IBR payments, any remaining debt is cancelled.

Check out all the rules at **http://studentaid.ed.gov/repay-loans/understand/plans/income-based** to see if you qualify.

— *Mandi L. Matlock, Austin*

Small
Talk

You're a lobbyist? How do you live with yourself?

Do you know Mr. X? He works at the capitol.

You know, my friends tell me I would be a great lobbyist. How do I become one?

Yes, I sleep well.

No, I don't know everyone who works at the Capitol, but I would like to meet him or her.

Really? Here's how . . . The truth is, there is no magic formula to become a lobbyist. The most common way is to have experience in the public sector, either in a legislative office or an agency. The easiest is to share consanguinity with an elected official. You do not need to be a lawyer or have a special degree. The only mandates call for yearly registration with the Texas Ethics Commission and subsequent financial reporting. There is no prototypical lobbyist. Anyone can be one. Don't believe me? Google Bill "Sputnik" Strain—arguably one of the greatest lobbyists in Texas history.

— David Courreges, Austin

how do I get out of it?

And while we're at it, how do I get out of paying taxes, getting my car inspected, and waiting in line at the Department of Motor Vehicles?

The short answer, of course, is that you can't legally avoid jury duty simply because you don't want to participate. Section 62.109 of the Government Code does allow exemptions for certain individuals, if they wish, including those who—

- are over seventy years of age;
- have legal custody of a child younger than ten years of age and the person's service on the jury requires leaving the child without adequate supervision;
- are a student of a public or private secondary school or attending an institution of higher education;

- are an officer or an employee of the senate, house of representatives, or any department, commission, board, office, or other agency in the legislative branch of government;
- have recently served as a petit juror, though the time periods vary by county; or
- are the primary caretaker of a person who is an invalid unable to care for himself (excluding health care workers).

Federal courts have somewhat different rules, and the standards for demonstrating a legitimate hardship vary from court to court. While most judges are sympathetic to those for whom jury service would create serious difficulties, it is also true that judges aren't stupid—they've heard it all. Claiming a hardship that you don't actually have is likely to result in unfortunate consequences.

Lawyers have a special responsibility to educate the public about the legal system, so here's your opportunity to do so. Tell them that trial by jury is a fundamental tenet of a democratic society that depends upon its citizens undertaking this obligation. Tell them how juries should reflect all walks of life and that allowing privileged groups to opt out of service could substantially alter the quality and integrity of legal verdicts. Although jury service frequently is viewed as inconvenient, explain how jurors often find the solemn responsibility of rendering a verdict for real people with real disputes far more interesting, enlightening, and rewarding than they expected.

Finally, tell them that if they are ever wrongfully accused of a crime or find themselves in litigation, they will be thankful that twelve of their fellow citizens have taken the time and effort to listen to give them a full and fair hearing of their case.

— *Jonathan E. Smaby, Austin*

Can an airline prohibit me from boarding an airplane if I am wearing a provocative outfit?

Technically, yes. An airline's "contract of carriage" typically allows it to refuse to board a passenger if the passenger's appearance could offend reasonable sensibilities of other passengers to the point of causing an onboard disturbance. But such instances are rare. Today's airlines operate in a complex environment, but safety is most important.

Perceptions about clothing are necessarily framed by one's subjective point of view rather than objective standards, so different people will respond or react differently. Whether an outfit is provocative, offensive, or just plain unsuitable enough to lead to an onboard disturbance is hard to predict.

Although it would take an extreme situation for an airline to refuse to board you, it's always best to wear something on board an airplane that won't require airline personnel to make a judgment.

— *Kelli Jones, Houston*

I am a parent of a two-year-old child. My husband and I often go out to eat with our son. One restaurant did not allow us to eat there because the business does not allow children.

Can children be prohibited from a restaurant?

It surprises many people to know that restaurants can prohibit almost anyone from dining at their establishment. The few exceptions include those classes that are protected by the U.S. Constitution or by statute, including race, gender, sexual orientation, religion, national origin, disability, and veteran status.

You might think that keeping children out could fall under the age exception, but it does not. The age exception applies only to the elderly. Therefore, a restaurant may prohibit children. Bars and nightclubs do this all the time, and restaurants are no different.

— *Matthew M. Sanderson, Dallas*

lawsuit! How can these frivolous lawsuits result in such huge awards?

The McDonald's "hot coffee case" is anything but a story of frivolous litigation. Even the current proprietary owner of the "Stella Awards," who is no friend of lawsuits or lawyers, acknowledges that much of the folklore that has sprung up around this case "has been grossly unfair." The truth is that after seventy-nine year-old Stella Liebeck spilled a cup of McDonald's coffee into her lap, suffering second and third degree burns to her thighs and pelvic region and requiring hospitalization, skin grafting, and two years of follow-up treatment, she and her lawyers discovered that prior to this incident, McDonald's had received over seven hundred reports of similar burn incidents caused by spills of its coffee.

And Ms. Liebeck was not anxious to sue anybody. Initially, she wrote a letter to McDonald's requesting only three things: (1) an explanation or investigation as to how this could have happened, (2) a reevaluation or change to coffee temperature policies and procedures to prevent this happening to other customers, and (3) payment of out of pocket medical and other incidental expenses, only to the extent they were not covered by Medicare. She had no lawyer.

McDonald's refused all of Ms. Liebeck's requests and instead offered her a lump sum payment of $800 if she would give the company a full and complete release. By then, her medical expenses were several thousand dollars. Flustered, Ms. Liebeck hired attorney Reed Morgan, and he sent a written demand for $90,000, including compensation for pain and suffering, scarring and disfigurement, and medical and related expenses. This offer to settle was also rejected, and Morgan then filed suit. Just before trial, after amassing substantial evidence of McDonalds' negligence and of Ms. Liebeck's damages, Ms. Liebeck and her lawyer offered to settle for $300,000, and an independent mediator recommended that McDonald's pay $225,000.

At the trial, McDonald's quality control manager testified that any beverage over 130 degrees in temperature constituted a burn hazard, that McDonald's coffee as served was not fit for human consumption, and that he personally knew what kind of damage it could cause from having viewed photographs of prior scalding injuries, but that neither he nor the company had done anything to change company policies.

The jury found McDonald's 80 percent responsible for the accident and Stella Liebeck 20 percent responsible and awarded $200,000 in compensatory damages, which were then reduced by Ms. Liebeck's 20 percent responsibility for her own injury under New Mexico law. This resulted in an actual damages judgment of $160,000. However, because of the testimony indicating that even seven hundred prior burn injuries had not caused McDonald's to reevaluate the temperature at which it served coffee and because the company knew the danger associated with such a high serving temperature, the jury also awarded $2.7 million in exemplary damages based on the amount of revenue generated by McDonald's from selling coffee in all its stores for two days. As was within his discretion, the trial judge quickly reduced the punitive damages to $480,000. The final judgment was for a total of $640,000, and McDonald's, of course, appealed rather than pay it. The case was settled between the parties for less than $600,000. McDonald's ignored reasonable settlement demands both before and after Ms. Liebeck hired a lawyer, and they ignored the independent and accurate evaluation of a neutral mediator. They gambled and they lost.

Sadly, Stella Liebeck lived the last years of her life not as a respected victim who successfully persevered in bringing corporate America to justice, but as a national disgrace, all because she humbly asked a company to behave more safely and to reimburse her preventable expenses and because she wouldn't abandon her quest even after years of aggravation.

*— **William J. Chriss, Austin***